Children's Clothes

A Water Carrier

Men's Hats

A Tudor Merchant

Ladies' Head-Dresses

A Ladybird Book
Series 561

Henry VIII was very popular with his subjects at the beginning of his reign. He was young, handsome, friendly with everybody, and athletic. But he was selfish, and when unable to get what he wanted, very cruel. He was, however, a patriotic Englishman and we have much to thank him for today.

© LADYBIRD BOOKS LTD 1973
All rights reserved. No part of this publication may be reproduced, stored in a retrieval system, or transmitted in any form or by any means, electronic, mechanical, photo-copying, recording or otherwise, without the prior consent of the copyright owner.

Henry VIII

by L. DU GARDE PEACH,
O.B.E., M.A., Ph.D., D.Litt.

with illustrations by
FRANK HUMPHRIS

Ladybird Books Ltd Loughborough

HENRY VIII, 1491-1547

Most people know that Henry VIII of England was married six times, and that he was the father of Queen Elizabeth I. There was, however, a great deal more to Henry than that.

He was born at Greenwich in 1491, nearly five hundred years ago, when England was very different from the country it is today. There were only about three million inhabitants, most of whom were farmers. There were no great cities or factories, the roads were very bad indeed, and the quickest way of getting from one place to another was either on horse-back or in a clumsy, horse-drawn carriage without springs. In winter the roads were often so deep in mud that travelling was avoided as much as possible.

The English were great sailors, but the biggest ships were no more than about one thousand tons. The Spanish ship *Santa Maria* in which Columbus sailed to America was only one hundred tons. All were, of course, sailing ships, built of wood: voyages took many weeks, during which time the sailors were quite out of touch with land.

When Columbus sailed on one of the most historically important voyages of all time, Henry Tudor, the future King Henry VIII of England, was only a few weeks over one year old. His father, Henry VII, had been asked, but had refused, to contribute money towards the venture. This lost for England the chance of being the first European country to claim America.

0 7214 0352 2

Prince Henry grew up to be a very attractive and handsome young man. He excelled at many sports. It was said of him that he could draw a long-bow of greater strength than any other man in England. He was famous for his wrestling, and for hunting the stags which were then common in the woods and on the wild moors: he played tennis and in mock battles, known as jousting, he was a formidable opponent.

Henry was the second son of Henry VII, and it was not unusual for the younger son of a monarch to hold a high position in the Church. England was then, of course, a Catholic country. It is strange to think that Prince Henry might well have become a Prince Cardinal, possibly even the Pope of Rome. The whole history of England and of Europe would have been very different if his elder brother, Prince Arthur, had not died at the age of sixteen. Henry became heir to the throne when he was eleven years old.

His education had been that of both prince and priest. He spoke French, Italian, Spanish and Latin, and was skilled in music. He played various instruments and composed songs, some of which are still sung today. He studied theology and later wrote essays for which the Pope granted him the title of 'Defender of the Faith', long retained on British coinage.

Henry was fond of children and could be jovial and friendly with all men: everyone looked forward to a truly merry England when he succeeded to the throne.

If you had been invited to have your dinner with young Prince Henry, you would have been surprised at the various and strange things you were given to eat, and you would have looked in vain for a fork with which to eat them. Each guest was provided with a bowl of water and a napkin: these were for washing and wiping the fingers from time to time when they became sticky and messy.

Your knife would be in your belt and used for all purposes: at the end of the meal you wiped it on the hem of your tunic. As for a spoon, in a fine household a wooden or pewter one was often provided by your host; otherwise you did without. In a palace you might have had a plate of silver or even of gold: the usual thing was a pewter platter, and sometimes you had merely a thick slice of bread. This was both practical and economical. It soaked up the gravy and the juice, and at the end of the meal you ate it. There was then no washing up!

The meals provided for the nobles and the richer people were enormous, and chiefly of meat or poultry. There were no potatoes, but better varieties of cabbages and beans were introduced into this country by Henry's gardeners.

The Romans had grown many kinds of fruit in England, but these had died out after the Roman legions left. They were re-introduced by the royal gardeners: cherries, plums and apricots, gooseberries and strawberries were brought from Holland to flourish in English soil.

It would be very tedious to attempt to explain all the little wars and treaties in Europe in the days of Henry VII. He had been a very crafty man, careful with his money and very unwilling to waste it on fighting one country after another, all to no purpose.

In those days kings and queens were absolute monarchs: this means that they ruled their countries in any way they pleased; there was no way of forbidding them, other than by a revolution. This led to many strange alliances and treaties, few of which were ever kept by the monarchs who signed them. These alliances often involved a marriage between a prince and princess of the two countries concerned. The young princesses and princes had no say in the matter.

The two most powerful countries in Europe at that time were France and Spain. So when Henry VII signed a treaty with Spain, his eldest son, Prince Arthur was involved. The Spanish princess was Catherine of Aragon, and they were married when Arthur was fifteen and Catherine almost a year older.

Unfortunately Arthur died in the following year, and Prince Henry became the future King of England. Arthur's widow, Catherine, was married to Henry on the death of his father Henry VII, in 1509. This was against all the rules of the Church, and the wishes of the people of England, who hated the Spaniards. The Pope was persuaded to give his permission for the marriage, together with his blessing for the future happiness of the young couple.

When he became King, Henry had ample scope for the two sides of his strange nature. It was said of him that he seemed like a combination of two men; one, the merry, jovial monarch, fond of banquets and shows, who could play happily with children for hours: the other a man of restless energy and great ferocity. His unfortunate advisers never knew which to expect, the patron of sport and music, or the obstinate statesman determined to get his own way at all costs. Life was very difficult for them.

In many ways Henry was the right sort of king for England at a time when only a ruthless and adventurous monarch could hope to achieve anything in the complicated affairs of Europe. In other ways he was a bad king and a bad man, cruel and heartless.

His choice of the men who became his chief councillors made it clear that he was not prepared to trust what was left of the old nobility, most of whom had been killed during the Wars of the Roses, or at the Battle of Bosworth which had made Henry VII the King of England. If they opposed him, he had a short way of dealing with those nobles who remained.

Henry's chief and cleverest adviser was Cardinal Wolsey, the son of a butcher who had been convicted of selling meat unfit for human consumption. Another was Thomas Cromwell, an unknown lawyer. They served the King faithfully, but their reward was his selfish ingratitude.

Henry was fearless, and he was as tireless as he was brave. On a day's hunting over the wild moors and in the vast forests of England, he would often exhaust eight or ten horses, and his attendants found it impossible to keep up with him.

When they found him, he was likely to be sitting on a stile by a collection of squalid hovels, with his horse grazing nearby. Henry would be talking and laughing with a group of serfs, naturally and without embarrassment. The result was that he understood the common people, their thoughts and grievances, far better than did the nobles. It is not surprising that he was known to his subjects as Bluff King Hal.

Another and more important result was that they loved and trusted him. His massive body and his skill at all kinds of sport, no less than his jovial laugh and obvious friendliness, ensured his safety better than an armed guard. He went everywhere, often alone, riding the winding woodland paths and the rough country roads. The serfs working on the land knew him by his flaming red hair, and they felt that he was the right kind of king for them.

Henry, like King Alfred before him, realised that the safety of England depended upon the sea. The only land frontier which was dangerous was that between England and Scotland. A Welshman himself, he did not expect trouble from Wales. The Scots were different: they were a race of tough, fighting men.

Henry's father had already taken precautions against the Scots. He had married his daughter, Margaret, to King James IV of Scotland, a marriage which was later to affect the whole history of Britain. It did not, however, prevent the Scots from invading England, resulting in the Battle of Flodden Field, in which King James IV was killed. Henry was not present at the Battle of Flodden. He was fighting a not very successful war in France.

Henry took every opportunity to talk with sailors and visit the ports. Ships were built, already one of them, the *Henri Grâce à Dieu*, also known as the *Great Harry*, was as much as 1,500 tons. It was the largest warship afloat, and had seven decks: it out-gunned any other ship of its period. Nevertheless during the reign of Henry's daughter, Elizabeth, when the English beat off the Spanish Armada, it was the seamanship of the English sailors, rather than the size of the Navy, which won the day.

Henry took a close personal interest in the ships which were being built. He always believed that he knew more than the experts and, as he was often right, it kept them hard at work. There was no slackness under this young vigorous king. If a new ship was found to sail slowly, he had to know the reason why: if it was proved to be the fault of a careless shipwright, Henry made certain that he would never do it again.

Henry came to the throne in 1509. It was a time of progress and discovery; map-making and navigation had been advanced by the efforts of the Portuguese Prince Henry; the new art of printing had been brought to England by Caxton and, in war, the practical use of gunpowder had been discovered.

After King Richard III had been killed at the Battle of Bosworth, in 1485, life in England began to change, slowly but surely. Henry VIII began his reign at a favourable time to benefit from the new inventions and the opportunities which they presented.

Henry's father had been very careful not to waste money, and very good at accumulating it. So, at the age of eighteen, young Henry found himself with a great fortune entirely at his disposal. He was very ready to spend it. His love of every kind of extravagant show, from personal clothes and jewels to pageants and banquets, soon began to waste the money in a way which would have horrified his careful father.

At what became known as 'The Field of the Cloth of Gold' he had every opportunity for display. It was staged as a show by Henry to impress the French King. The rich colours of Henry's robes, the brilliantly decorated tents of the English nobles and statesmen, the banquets and the medieval pageantry of the jousting, all certainly achieved their aim of impressive splendour, but they failed in their real purpose. Henry of England and Francis of France became no more friendly than they had been before.

The famous Cardinal Wolsey played a great part in the changes which were beginning to affect England. He was twenty years older than Henry, an amusing and witty companion and a cunning and unscrupulous adviser. He had an iron constitution, and was able to revel all night with the young King before going straight on to twenty-four hours of hard and brilliant work in his office, without any sign of strain or lack of energy. He was exactly the kind of man to impress Henry.

Wolsey did not fail to profit from the King's favour. In those days a man looked for his reward in two ways: either by rising to high rank in the Church, which cost the King nothing, or by being given an office such as Collector of Taxes, with all its opportunities of wealth, or even as Chancellor, which offered more.

Wolsey looked in both directions. He became a bishop, and soon after that, Archbishop of York: the high honour of being a Cardinal of the Catholic Church came to him by the time Henry had been six years on the throne.

For most churchmen this would have been sufficient reward, but not for Cardinal Wolsey. He was too able and too industrious to be satisfied with the administration of church affairs. In the same year he was appointed Lord Chancellor of England. Short of becoming King, this son of a rascally butcher could get no higher. He built wonderful houses, including Hampton Court, where he lived in greater state than the King himself and is said to have had a thousand servants. It is not surprising that the members of the old nobility hated him.

In spite of the fortune left by his careful father, Henry needed more money to pay for the French Wars and for his extravagant habits. Within a year of becoming King he had made himself popular by executing two men, Empson and Dudley, who had been hated for levying taxes under Henry VII. He now found himself obliged to do as they had done. Wolsey helped by devising new taxes, but although these raised a great deal of money, not all of it found its way to the King! Wolsey was an expensive servant!

In the meantime Henry had other problems. He wanted a son who could succeed him on the throne, but he had only a daughter, Mary. So he decided to marry someone younger than Queen Catherine, which meant he would have to divorce her. But divorce was not possible without the approval of the Supreme Head of the Catholic Church, the Pope.

The difficulty was this: the Pope had reluctantly given special permission for Henry to marry the widow of Prince Arthur. To approach the Papal Court with a demand for a divorce, was as good as saying that the Pope had been wrong. England was a Catholic country and every Catholic knew and believed that the Pope could never be wrong. To expect him to change his decision was going too far.

In those days the Pope was not only the Head of the Catholic Church; he was also the ruler of part of Italy. As such he was in a very difficult position. Catherine of Aragon was the aunt of the Spanish King, who angrily sent an army into Italy and captured Rome. There was nothing the Pope could do except to refuse to listen to Wolsey, who had been sent by Henry to obtain the Pope's agreement to a divorce.

Henry was furious, and his anger was directed chiefly against Cardinal Wolsey. It was not Wolsey's fault, but he had already told Henry confidently that there would be no difficulty. He had to return to London and inform Henry that there was no hope of agreement; the Pope was a prisoner in the hands of the Spanish King.

Henry was determined to marry a young maid-of-honour named Anne Boleyn, the daughter of a wealthy London merchant. She had been well educated—partly in France—and was a good musician; but she was ambitious and unscrupulous. When she realised that she had attracted the attentions of Henry, she was determined to become Queen at any cost. Perhaps if she had known that the cost was to be her head, she might have hesitated.

Although this marriage was important to Anne, the importance to England was infinitely greater. Not only did it bring about the fall of Wolsey, one of the greatest of English statesmen, it changed the religious life of the people of England.

The negotiations with the Pope and with Spain about the divorce of Catherine dragged on for six years. Finally Henry decided that marriage with Anne was more important than the blessing of the Pope, and declared himself Head of the Church of England. As the divorce of Catherine now depended only on the King himself, he lost no time in marrying Anne Boleyn. Wolsey had already been deprived of everything except the Archbishopric of York. When later he was summoned to London to be tried on a false charge, he died on the way, at Leicester.

Henry's marriage to Anne, and the disgrace of Wolsey, may appear unimportant to us today, until we remember that Anne and Henry's daughter became Queen Elizabeth I, and England became a Protestant country.

Henry's desire to marry Anne Boleyn was not the only reason why England ceased officially to be a Catholic country. Henry needed money. He saw that the immediate answer to his problem was to seize the wealth of the monasteries, now no longer under the protection of the Pope. Henry was not slow to realise that while taxes were unpopular, many of the monasteries were even more so.

In earlier centuries the monasteries had served a useful purpose. They had been hospitals for the sick and hostels for travellers; they had helped the poor and taught the ignorant; they had comforted the sorrowful and protected the innocent. But by the time Henry came to the throne there were schools and universities, other inns and hospitals of sorts, and local justices and law-courts. The monasteries had become immensely rich and the monks fat and lazy. Few people were sorry to see them closed down.

The dissolution of the monasteries was useful to Henry in another way. In the course of time, rich men had left land to them, and many of the monasteries possessed very large estates. These were now confiscated by the King and given to those whom he wished to reward. There are families in England today who have inherited, from generation to generation, estates which were once owned and farmed by the monasteries. The Pope excommunicated Henry, which meant that he was deprived of the rites of the Church. Henry ignored the Pope and went on exactly as before.

In the meantime Henry was taking no chances. He allowed the clergy to pass any new laws governing the Church, providing he approved. However, such laws were not to be the law of the land, and anyone who acted on them in the belief that they were, could be in serious trouble. The election of bishops, which had previously depended upon the Pope, was to be the free choice of the canons of the Cathedral. They received a licence to elect a bishop, accompanied by a letter from the King telling them *whom* to elect.

It had been the custom for the first year's income of a newly-elected bishop to be paid, not to the bishop, but to the Pope. As these payments came to thousands of pounds Henry insisted that anything which had previously been paid to the Pope must now come to him. Very few sources of money escaped Henry's attention.

But increased taxes became necessary and the north of England rose in revolt. It was now that the merciless ferocity of Henry's character began to show itself. The country was said to have been dotted with the gibbets from which hung the bodies of those who had dared to defy the King.

The revolt had been most savagely crushed, but the main cause of it remained. This was Thomas Cromwell, now chief minister and favourite adviser of the King. Cromwell's spies were everywhere, and he kept in Henry's favour by bringing him daily reports of plots—true or false—threatening the King's life.

Thomas Cromwell (not to be confused with Oliver Cromwell, who lived more than a hundred years later), had a beginning even less promising than Wolsey's. He was obliged to leave England at an early age and was in France and Italy by the time he was eighteen. Whether he followed his father's supposed trade as a blacksmith is not known, and there is no record of his education. All that we do know is that he was naturally as clever as he was unscrupulous.

He returned to England at a time when Wolsey was becoming powerful. After trading as a money-lender, an occupation he had learned in Florence from the great money-lenders of Europe, he entered the service of Cardinal Wolsey. Soon we find him reporting on the state of the monasteries and winning the favour of Henry by his zeal in suppressing them. The King was even more grateful when Cromwell suggested that instead of wasting more time arguing with the Pope, Henry should declare himself Head of the Church of England.

When Wolsey fell into disgrace, Cromwell was the only man who remained faithful to him, which was very much to his credit. He had nothing more to hope for from Wolsey, but he had not forgotten that he owed so much to the fallen cardinal.

When Wolsey died at Leicester, everyone else had deserted him. Wolsey had nothing left to give except advice. If Cromwell had followed it, he might not have lost his head on Tower Hill. He lived simply, whereas Wolsey had been grossly extravagant, but he became even more powerful than his former master had ever been.

When Henry's marriage with Anne Boleyn produced only a daughter, his conscience conveniently began to trouble him. He suddenly realised that he had committed a sin in divorcing Catherine and marrying Anne Boleyn. The truth was that he had become tired of her, and desired to marry a rather silly young woman named Jane Seymour. Feeling that another divorce so soon would not be popular, the cruelty of his nature was clearly shown when he caused poor Anne to be executed.

Anne Boleyn had lasted three years as Henry's queen: Jane Seymour lasted only a year, and was probably fortunate in dying before Henry became tired of her also. She was attractive, but brainless, with none of Anne Boleyn's wit. However, she gave Henry the son he so much desired, the future Edward VI.

Henry next strengthened his position as Head of the Church by causing an English translation of the Bible to be printed, and a copy to be displayed in every church. Even though printing had been introduced into England by Caxton sixty years earlier, this was a very large task. Nevertheless in every place of worship, from St. Paul's Cathedral down to the smallest parish church, people read it or had it read to them.

Previously the contents of the New Testament had not been available to the common people. Now they were able to read or hear about Christ's concern for the poor and needy. Those who were not poor and needy— the nobles—supported Henry because most of them had been given land confiscated from the monasteries. They had no intention of giving it back.

One marriage of Henry's, that with Anne Boleyn, had brought about the fall of Wolsey: another, with Anne of Cleves, had the same result for Cromwell.

The two most powerful Catholic countries in Europe, France and Spain, had become friends and allies. Cromwell was afraid that they might join together to attack England, and he wanted to have at least one friendly Protestant country in Europe. As Henry was now a widower, Cromwell looked around for an available Protestant princess. He found one named Anne of Cleves.

He arranged for her portrait, by the famous painter Holbein, to be sent to Henry. This portrait made Anne of Cleves appear to be very beautiful, and Henry looked forward to meeting her. But first he wanted a private view, so he went in disguise to the Crown Inn at Rochester, where Anne was to stay for a few hours. When he saw her, so unlike the portrait which Cromwell had shown him, he was furious.

Henry turned angrily on Cromwell and we can guess what he said. He likened poor Anne to a "great Flanders mare" and although he was obliged to marry her, a separation was quickly arranged. Anne was lucky. She was given an estate and a pension on condition that she did not use the title of Queen. She had no wish to do anything except to live an idle life, working at her tapestries and eating far too much, so this suited both of them. Henry was now free to marry his fifth wife, Catherine Howard, and did so the same year. If she really knew what had happened to the other four, Catherine Howard was either a brave or a foolish woman.

By this time Henry was almost fifty and had lost all his youthful good looks and charm. He was immensely fat through over-eating, bald, and in constant pain. This did not improve his temper, and anyone who approached him did so with fear and trembling. To oppose him meant almost certain execution.

Catherine Howard was a pampered, irresponsible girl. She could not see the danger of being surrounded by jealous enemies when married to a brute who was always ready to listen to scandalous rumours. However, Henry felt better in the spring, and a magnificent progress (tour) to the north of England was arranged. The weather was bad, the roads were often impassable, and many weeks were wasted. The delays did not worry Catherine. She was foolish enough to arrange to meet former lovers in secret on the way north.

Whether Catherine had wanted to marry Henry is doubtful. A young girl of the nobility was often forced to play a part in the game of politics. Catherine was a Howard, and the family, including the Duke of Norfolk, used her to influence the King. She failed to do so and when he learned of her unfaithfulness, Henry had her executed.

By this time he was broken in health and in spirit, old and worn. When it was suggested that he should marry again as a matter of policy, he angrily refused. Yet Henry, ruthless, bloated and racked with constant pain, felt the need of a companion. His last and sixth wife, Catherine Parr, brought him the comfort and care of which he was so much in need.

Many people think of Henry the Eighth as a man constantly occupied in marrying, divorcing or beheading one wife after another. This is to take an entirely wrong view of a king who was perhaps more unfortunate than wicked. That he *was* wicked in some ways there is no doubt, but he had a strong religious faith, and always believed he was doing his best for England.

In his treatment of Thomas Cromwell he was unjust to a man who, in an age of dishonesty, was more honest than most. Cromwell had been raised by Henry to become Vicar-General, a sort of second-in-command to the Head of the Church. Many civilian honours were bestowed on him. He was created Baron Cromwell and a Knight of the Garter, and it was as the Lord Great Chamberlain of England that he arranged the marriage of the King with Anne of Cleves. In doing so he was serving England, rather than seeking to please Henry, and this was his mistake.

However, it was not this mistake which caused his immediate downfall; he was created Earl of Essex in the same year. It was a charge of treason brought by the Duke of Norfolk, who hated him, which finally caused him to be beheaded. He never had a fair trial: in those days just a charge of treason was enough.

Some historians have insisted that Cromwell was a ruffian with no regard for anything sacred. This is unjust to a man who was only trying to carry out the policy of his master, the King, with the greatest efficiency.

Caxton, the first English printer, died in the year in which Henry VIII was born. His press had been set up at Westminster some fifteen years earlier. By the time Henry became King, it had produced hundreds of books.

In the days before Caxton, when it was decided to make a number of copies of a book, one monk read it aloud while twenty or thirty others wrote it down. Some of the monks may have been deaf and wrote what they thought they heard; some could not spell, and some were simply lazy or careless. Consequently no two copies were ever alike, and some were very bad indeed.

Printing altered all this. A hundred or even a thousand copies of a book could be made by two or three men. These copies were exactly alike, without the mistakes caused by careless or ignorant copying. The monks, seeing their pleasant peaceful occupation threatened, hated the printers and their presses.

A far more serious threat to the early printers was that some people feared there was a danger to the State through the spread of ideas. Many pious churchmen called for the destruction of the presses before it was too late. "Content is gone from the world," they said. "Men would be quick to use this new miracle of printing for evil, rather than for good." They insisted that not only was the printed word a danger to the State, but it could easily be used to spread the heresies of those who differed from the official doctrine of what was then a Catholic England.

If you were to see a page of a book, printed in English, by William Caxton, you might have difficulty in reading it. The letters were what is called Gothic type today. Many of the words have disappeared from our language.

When books became more easily available, some of the common people learned to read. Because all books had previously been laboriously copied by hand, they had been few and costly. Now there were many more for those able to read. This was the beginning of what was known as the New Learning.

The art of printing changed not only England, but the world. It brought new thoughts to simple people. Men and women had been more or less contented with the way they thought God had ordained that they should live—the lord in his castle and the peasant in his hut. But now they began to wonder whether this was right.

There had been poems such as *Piers Plowman*, and rough plays such as *The Shepherds' Play*, written before printing came to England. But the poems were copied by hand and the plays were often moral lessons or stories from the Bible. They were performed by priests or by the trade guilds.

There were, of course, no theatres in these early days. The scenes were played on large wagons, dragged from street to street and sometimes they were simply knock-about horse-play. Often the actors were persecuted and made to sit in the stocks. But they made people think. When they began to think they began to question the right of some people to be rich, with plenty to eat and good warm clothes to wear. This was the beginning of much discontent in the country.

But as I sleep me mette
Within a temple y-m...
In whiche ther were ...
Of gold stondinge i...
And mo riche tabe...
And with perree ...
...eynt ma...

Photography was not invented until hundreds of years after the time of Henry VIII. The possibility of colour photography, which would have shown us the true colour of Henry's beard, had not been even imagined.

But there have always been men who could paint lakes or landscapes, buildings or ships. The earliest civilisations have left portraits of great men, sometimes in paint, sometimes as coloured statues or mosaics. From these we are able to obtain an idea of what men looked like hundreds and even thousands of years ago.

Having no cameras, rich men who travelled abroad in their own private carriages, attended by servants and valets, coachmen and footmen, always included an artist. He was a living camera, his job being to make a record of whatever seemed of particular interest to the rich nobleman. The Bridge of Sighs, in Venice, and the Colosseum, in Rome, were painted by the travelling artists then, just as they are photographed by enthusiastic American tourists today.

These men were not always skilled artists, but in Henry's day there were some great portrait painters, such as Holbein and Titian. Two miniatures of Catherine Howard and Anne of Cleves exist, neither very exciting; Anne Boleyn, pictured in the National Portrait Gallery, looks neither beautiful nor intelligent. A portrait of Catherine Parr is of a motherly-looking woman with a somewhat cautious expression. Probably as Henry's wife she had need of caution!

Portraits of men in Henry's time are better than those of women. For some reason the women all look similar to one another, with mask-like faces, mostly lacking in expression. The fact that many of the men wore beards made it easier. If the painter gets the shape and colour of a beard right he is half-way towards getting a recognisable likeness.

There is a magnificent portrait by Holbein of Henry VIII in St. James's Palace, Westminster. It is exactly what everybody imagines Henry VIII looked like. Holbein was a very great portrait painter and he was painting from life.

Portraits of Wolsey and Thomas Cromwell, both in the National Portrait Gallery, look stern and determined, as indeed these men were. Both are beardless, but the painter has caught expressions of ruthless ambition combined with extreme cunning. It was an age when the task of a statesman was to deceive.

In some periods of history, beards were considered the mark of the manly hero: in others they were the sign of beggars and holy men. Hair was sometimes long, sometimes short, according to the fashion, set by some popular hero or the whim of the monarch himself. Henry's father, the first of the Tudors, was clean-shaven, but his hair was long: Henry himself grew a red beard. At the request of his wife, he shaved it off, but grew it again before going to 'The Field of the Cloth of Gold'. The beard greatly impressed the French on that memorable occasion.

Although most of us go through life without breaking the law seriously, we know that those who do, risk appearing before a local magistrate. They may be punished or fined for small offences: in the case of more serious crimes, they are passed on to higher courts to appear before a judge.

Of course there had always been law of a sort in England. At first it was rough, and only too ready to condemn the poor man whilst sparing the rich. As time went on the law became more reasonable. By the time of King John, Magna Carta laid it down that a man must be judged by his peers. This did not mean the nobility, but men like himself, whose way of life was similar.

This wise law, the very basis of freedom, had been much abused. There were ways of avoiding it, which clever lawyers were not slow to discover. If a nobleman was powerful enough, he simply ignored it. Under the first two Tudors, Henry VIII and his father, the powers of the local magistrates were strengthened and abuses of the higher courts were put right.

But, at a time when there were no regular police, there were many robbers and thieves of all sorts. If they were able to bribe the right people, they were reasonably safe from the law. Now, life and property were made safer by the new powers of the courts and of the Judges of Assize, as the judges who visited all parts of the country in turn were called.

No English king has been more praised and more hated than Henry VIII. Some historians regard him as a good king, ready to help the poor and to be friendly with men of all kinds. He was, they say, educated and reasonable; he was fond of music and poetry; he was good company, witty and intelligent.

Other historians see Henry as a brutal man, unfit to mix with decent people, who should have been shut up as mad, or put in prison, long before he died.

Both opinions are right, up to a point. There was much in what Henry achieved for which we should be grateful to this day. If it had not been for his quarrel with the Pope, this country might have been devastated by a disastrous civil war. It is true that his motives were often wrong, but he was a fiercely patriotic Englishman.

As a young king he had every advantage. He was handsome, popular with all classes, a good athlete, cultured and good-natured with everybody. It is probable that if he had been able to settle down as a family man with his first wife, Catherine of Aragon, and had a family as handsome, intelligent, and as good at sports as he was himself, he would be remembered as one of the best monarchs England ever had. Fate was against him. He was quick-tempered and had absolute power. It was a fatal combination. It has been wisely said that power tends towards evil, and the greater the power, the greater the evil. Henry VIII was an example of the truth of this.

The 'Henri Grâce à Dieu'
or the 'Great Harry'

Watches
of the
1540's

Tudor Window
showing typical flat arch